"Mike James is a poet in love with bridges, a poet of praise in search of connective tissue, relentlessly on the move, searching for signifiers, trying to find that loose thread of inspiration. "The sky is something we can drink from," he writes. "Darkness is never clean or clear," knowing a human being in love with mystery is never finished, and that the world is mostly hidden from us, and poetry is one of the ways humans discover the most important aspects of themselves, illuminating and untangling as it tells. These lovely poems are a blessing, an unexpected warm wind blows through them and amazing declarations shiver forth as James travels and watches and listens. "Sound brings us to our senses," said Thoreau, and the poems here are quiet and tight, acutely aware of their own dissolution, and the temporary spaces that we occupy. "The moon looks nothing like the one I touched," writes James, and with a deft surrealistic brush he fills in all the colors he finds and the ones he had hoped to find. There are wonders to discover in every poem and I gobbled them up. Sit with this book and listen and the singing will settle in your imagination. Don't just take my word for it, open the cover and start swimming and you will be immersed in a better world."

-Keith Flynn, editor of *The Asheville Poetry Review*
and author of *The Skin of Meaning*

**Other Books by Mike James:**

*Red Dirt Souvenir Shop*, Analog Submissions, 2020
*Journeyman's Suitcase,* Luchador, 2020
*Parades*, Alien Buddha, 2019
*Jumping Drawbridges in Technicolor,* Blue Horse, 2019
*First-Hand Accounts from Made-Up Places,*
Stubborn Mule, 2018
*Crows in the Jukebox, Bottom Dog*, 2017
*My Favorite Houseguest,* FutureCycle, 2017
*Peddler's Blues,* Main Street Rag, 2016
*The Year We Let the House Fall Down,* Aldrich, 2015
*Elegy in Reverse,* Aldrich, 2014
*Past Due Notices: Poems 1991-2011,*
Main Street Rag, 2012
*Alternate Endings, Foothills,* 2007
*Nothing but Love,* Pathwise, 2004
*Pennies from an Empty Jar,* Another Thing, 2002
*All Those Goodbyes,* Talent House, 2001
*Not Here,* Green Bean, 2000

# Leftover Distances

Poems by Mike James

Luchador Press
Big Tuna, TX

Copyright © Mike James, 2021
First Edition: 1 3 5 7 9 10 8 6 4 2
ISBN: 978-1-952411-47-2
LCCN: 2021930789

Cover art: Heather Symmes
Author photo: Sophie James
All rights reserved. No part of this publication may be reproduced or transmitted in any form or by any means, electronic or mechanical, including photocopying, recording or by info retrieval system, without prior written permission from the author.

## Acknowledgments:

Some of these poems, often in different versions, appeared in the following journals:

*San Pedro River Review, As It Ought To Be Magazine, Rye Whiskey Review, Deuce Coupe, Blue Pepper, Trampoline, Bombfire, Gargoyle, Cajun Mutt, Pine Hills Review, Gasconade Review, Sonic Boom, Rusty Truck, Heroin Love Songs, Chiron Review, Otoliths, Chantarelle's Notebook, Gas, The Long Islander, Sublunary Review, Club Plum,* and in the chapbook, *Double Feature* (with John Dorsey), published by Analog Submission.

# TABLE OF CONTENTS

I.

Drunk Butterflies near the Missouri River / 1

Almost Autumn and Time to Go / 2

Falling As We Go / 4

Thinning Stars Along the River / 5

Degrees of Gray in Chester / 6

Letter to Joe Arcangelini, On Another Coast / 7

Water & Dirt, Darkness & Reaching / 8

Discount Ghazal of Everyday Saints / 9

So This Happens / 10


II.

Our First Annual Cross-Country Trip / 15

Leaving the Parking Lot of the Comfort Food Diner,
   West of Vegas / 16

Temporary Keys / 17

Edward Hopper Country / 18

In Another City / 19

Night Rain Piano / 20

A Private Moon, In a Private Sky / 21

Astronomers Sitting on Rocks / 22

Main Streets / 23

Household / 24

My River / 25

Every Summer Was Always the Same / 26

Summer Grammar / 27
Wind & Those Afterthoughts / 28
Once In A While / 29
Where I'm From / 30

III.
Fairy Tale, as a Girl was About to Dream / 33
Spring Day in the Provinces / 34
Hitchhiking Towards the Apocalypse / 36
Matchstick Hullaballoo / 37
The Election / 38
After the Liberation / 39
Communique / 40
The Spoils of War / 41
Doomsday Museum / 42
The Refugees / 43
Flags Forever at Half-Mast / 44
After the Deluge / 45
The Man in the Yellow Hat / 46
Not Knowing the Rules / 47
A History of Capitalism / 48
In Defense of Surrealism / 49
Self-Crucifixion / 50

IV.
People, I Know People / 53
Leigh / 54
Sailors / 55

13 Things Liz Knows Better Than Most / 56

That Same Vincent of Alehouse Fame / 57

Tommy E / 58

Lew Welch Going Into the Mountains
    with His Rifle / 59

Sorry / 60

Nights & Days / 61

V.

Acceptance Jubilee / 65

Anyway, It Was In October, I Think / 66

Greetings & All / 67

So Far Away From Tuscany / 68

My Given Name is Mike / 69

A Slow, Secret Life / 70

Away From the Spotlight, in the July Sun / 72

One of Those Times / 73

All the Things I've Got to Do / 74

Bright Red Calendar Marks / 75

Some Items Inside That Big Red Box Underneath
    Your Bed / 76

Some Fairies / 77

The Butterfly Mirror I Play Peek-A-Boo With / 78

Dog Sitting / 79

Autobiography, In Brief / 80

Epitaph / 81

It's Lovely, At Last / 82

# Leftover Distances

# I.

*in this trade we pay no wages*
                        Basil Bunting

# Drunk Butterflies near the Missouri River
*for Jason Ryberg*

*nothing but your blind, stupefied heart*
                    John Thompson

Lord, even without belief, today is enough. A little chant I
   say to myself.
Structured right, it is a hymn. Not even I like to hear my
   singing.

Yesterday, I almost got lost going home. I wasn't following
   the advice
Of every teacher: Pay attention! I got through school.
   Got home.

I drive when I'm lonely. Take a lot of back, dirt roads.
   Never found
A collapsed bridge in any river. My luck. That's what keeps
   me driving.

It's August. Heat takes up everything. I think of weather.
   Think of rain.
Nothing changes. It's still August. With or without the river.

I've always lived beside a river. Never once hopped across
   on rocks. I distrust currents.
Don't like darkness moving fast or slow. Will walk a long
   way to take a good bridge.

I've heard every cliché about home is true. I'll say that, smile
   stupidly.
I don't always watch how hard the wind blows. I keep going.
   I go.

## Almost Autumn and Time to Go

*exhausted from saying goodbye*
                        Shawn Pavey


Jesus didn't say much. Hard to speak when your words come out unsavory red.
People ask and ask. How many answers are a head shake or a long stare?

The tongue shapes the world as best it can. Tell me what I don't know. A long list.
Start with a's. Vowels carry us along, not always merrily. Our tongues click and cluck.

We say please to the fishhook when hungry. Please to the needle when sick.
Easy to forget the niceties. Hear that preacher curse when he falls in the dark.

Neighbors don't hear us. We don't listen to ourselves. Maybe we do and don't care.
Is that a conundrum, like: When is near far and far near? Almost never, unless it is.

Everything goes back to travel. Get to heaven or just over there. Some of us stay ready.
We live by love or fear. Maybe adventures are one street over. Maybe streets are empty.

The answer to travel is always not here. Grace might be in
    the very next town.
There might be room to spare. Sift along long enough,
    a few things get clear.

# Falling as We Go

> *uneasy at last*
> John Berryman

You go swimming with a smooth stone on your back. Heavy, but fits well.
Maybe call the stone, *wants*. Better yet, at your midpoint, call it, *years*.

What do you give up in middle-age? Desire? No. It lingers and won't leave.
It is a stain that stays. Or a knife kept loose in a sheath. An uncertain blade.

We take smaller steps as we age. Pretend that's a dance. In a way it is.
Two steps forward. One step back. That's a shuffle habit makes.

Curse the night. It doesn't change. The moon's half-dollar remains unspent.
The dark gives cheap cover for want. Ask Old Man Lot. It was always like this.

Your hands tell what's real. True when young and now. Gravity no longer a friend.
If you fall, you find what's near. Sometimes you call out. Sometimes you keep still.

## Thinning Stars, Along the River

*Heaven goes on without us.*
John Thompson

We feed ourselves river oysters. Try to find an old man's face lining any inner shell.
Dinner is an art project. And a drinking contest. A time to argue, loudly. An excuse.

Stuck with our change jars and our poor, back-of-the gas station penny tosses.
Still here, with barely a name. There's no well big enough for all our wishes.

Our mythologies made from childhood, broken hearts, nightmares, and game shows.
No master key for the myths. Each suffers the calendar, warms or cools with seasons.

At night we check the sky. Find the Big Dipper. Find the Little Dipper. Give up then.
The sky is something we can drink from. Often, we can't believe how polished it is.

No crow will ever carry a star across the sky. There's a myth if you want to make it.
Even with a well-lit moon, some things stay hidden. Darkness is never clean or clear.

## Degrees of Gray in Chester

Shadows are the main crop here, regardless the season.
They blossom at daylight, keep things hidden.
Any smile you get won't last longer than a thought.
Laugh too much, someone will start a rumor
About your mind
Or money
Or sister
Or, else, attach to you their own leftover dream.

Main Street hosts three second hand stores.
Each offers another neighbor's hand-me-downs.
At one, a girl you knew is now the woman
Behind the counter.
You kissed her badly, once.
Never got around to loving for more than that kiss.
Whatever beauty she had left with the mills.
Talk to her and she'll tell you what's not here.
Her voice sounds like a wish.

# Letter to Joe Arcangelini, On Another Coast

The coffee was delicious and the rain is good to see.
Add enough mornings, get a long life.
Is fake profundity what you meant to wake to?
Some mornings, the nearly true is all I can manage.
I look out the window and wait.
Hard rain scattered the birds.
How bare is the shelter of a leafless tree?
A little less than necessary, little more than nothing.
If you think absence tastes like air, you haven't breathed here.
The factories closed years ago, an old odor stays.
The blanket sky is tattered in gray places.
That blanket is older than today.
The clouds look younger and younger.

## Water & Dirt, Darkness & Reaching

I sold my boat because I was afraid of drowning. One way I handle fear is to add Distance. I can run fast across a field if a bear is chasing. I imagine many bears.

The first time I swam in a river I worried about silt. Drowning on dirt. Yes, it happens. Leaves gather in a river along with rain water, beer bottles, and lusty curses from men.

I only walk on nights when every star is out. There's nothing romantic about that.
My fear of the dark as deep as my height. All I know of the stars is the light they bring.

As a child if I called in the night no one came. That's not true. Darkness came
And stayed. I learned to whistle then. A cousin told me, whistling keeps fear away.

I fall into a well and fear keeps me there. The well-rope is the one string instrument
I play. The music I make, just for me. I gave up whistling years ago. It rings in my ears.

## Discount Ghazal of Everyday Saints

We might forage for back door secrets and elevator shoes. Decorate our houses
In flea market drapery to resemble a penny arcade. It's all done for emphasis.

Sometimes we wish we stayed as we were born: naked, careless of fat lines.
Some of us age into palm readers and call our fingerprints our greatest gifts.

Once, I knew a man who claimed he was double-crossed by angels and garbage men.
Every whisper resembled a yell. Despite it all, his mouth was framed by smile lines.

My town is known for orphanages, plus street corners occupied by sword swallowers. The last circus left months ago. Go by the unemployment office. There's always a line.

Most of my friends live with hallucinations. Reality is where they put their emphasis.
When we all gather we count gifts, naked or draped in the curtains of Scarlet O'Hara.

## So This Happens

If I believed in sunrises as a cure all for late night disagreements, I'd wake you
Early and call you to an east window. The two of us have almost outlived belief.

Rumi started out offering knowledge to any stranger in his path. He ended
Offering blessings. Is that how we change between morning and night?

One of the things I like about you is how you make halos
Seem like an affectation of angels and rock stars.

Your best friend says your eyes are blue. I always thought they were
Harvest green…the color of my favorite, flea market bought, t-shirt.

Some people don't like to get dirty. Others swan dive into any
Trash bin. You are in the middle register. One note either way.

I do everything quickly, even rush my love and anger. You take your
Time, set up house. I look over every fence, make up stories as I pass.

After all these years we ask the same questions again and, yes, again.

An old test answered in pencil. We ask…Which blank do you fill in?

# II.

*My answers are inadequate*
*To those demanding day and date.*

Dorothy Parker

## Our First Annual Cross-Country Road Trip

We ran out of sandwiches and the good potato salad.
We made spells from small town names.
On a toll bridge, my top hat flew out the passenger window.
It became a temporary boat in the river below.
Our coins got sugar sticky, stuck together in the cup holder sun.
We always thought we were headed west even when we weren't.
The roads were littered with old maps and chicken feathers.
In the mountains, we used a straight razor as a snowplow.
We picked up Sigmund Freud as a hitchhiker.
We didn't complain about his cigar smell.
In one valley, we put *Just Married* on the back windshield.
Down the road, the rain took care of the marriage.

## Leaving the Parking Lot of the Comfort Food Diner, West of Vegas

Even when you don't count highway license plates
Time passes at a constant rate.
That's ok.
Most of what we see is meant to be erased.

The desert is good at that.
Wait long enough, sand erases every page.
Drive far enough, nobody knows your name.

## Temporary Keys

What if every house key only worked for a little while?
What if one day each of us was locked out?
What if we always carried a down jacket for any cold night
    it happened?
What if our jacket became a blanket, then a pillow?
What if our jacket sleeves were colorful, substitute wings?

## Edward Hopper Country

This is where the long-term lonely take up residence.

Even on the quietest summer Sunday,
Main Street is overwhelmed with color.

Sunlight bleaches out every second chance.

## In Another City

The cricket in the corner we couldn't find
That cold room seemed so big
Then the clock broke
We only knew to guess time at sunrise
The wind kept blowing more than one way
We worried about rain and what we didn't bring
There was coffee after sunrise
We were still cold

## Night Rain Piano

The rain plays the piano best at night
If it is a black piano, grand as a summer thunderstorm
And the roof is off an ancient, wooden house
Where no other furniture is left
And the rain falls unopposed on the keys
So people in the few cars driving past
Slowly on a nearly flooded road
Wonder who ever played so well

A Private Moon, In a Private Sky


The moon I reached for wasn't the closest.
The moon I reached for can only be seen every third clear
    night.
Neil Armstrong never walked on the moon I reached for.
The moon I reached for hasn't one bit of man shoe dust.
No astronauts ever circled the moon I reached for.
The moon I reached for looks nothing like the one I
    touched.

## Astronomers Sitting on Rocks

Astronomers playing hopscotch with stars
Astronomers playing checkers with stars
Astronomers not playing chess with stars
Astronomers playing dominoes with stars
Astronomers using stars for crossword puzzle answers
Astronomers sitting on round rocks, in empty fields, thinking
    of new names for stars
Names like Dream Box, Yesterday, and Revere

## Main Streets

People walk down them and sometimes dream of going
    from drugstore to moon
And the few who circle the moon know some bankers to
    say hello to
And each banker wants a few acres of moon dust
A few ask to stake claims to stars

## Household

Coffee: Dark as crow's wings. And then there's steam. Steam goes up. Of course it does. Is that your wish? Ways to travel are more than one. Travel is leaving. Silly rabbit, of course it is. The animal world is out there. You and your cat are here.

Silence: A bitterness strongest in the morning. Is it a hangover from dreams? That's a first guess. You like first things. And you make a lot of guesses. At crosswords. At calendars. There are game shows you think you could win.

Garden: The squirrels don't fear you or the birds. You feed them well. The garden is a rectangle. Limits, defined. As shaggy as the grass around it or tool shed behind it. The tool shed came with the house. Original paint cans and updated cobwebs honeycomb the shelves.

## My River

You are the night river I try to cross.
The water rises and rises.
I am a shaky swimmer, at best.
The largest rocks stay hidden.
I never think about what's under the rocks.
I'm always swimming, swimming.

# Every Summer Was Always the Same

He'd eat butter sandwiches three times a day.
On Sunday, he'd check his blood pressure with a garden hose.
A Zen witch taught him that trick for a pack of smokes.
Afterwards, he turned the green garden hose into a Sunday lasso.
He would climb to the moon when he could find it.
He liked it there.
He liked the moon quiet.
It was up beyond dark clouds and among white stars.

## Summer Grammar

The ampersand loves to drive around in an old yellow convertible, top down, semicolon in the passenger seat. The semicolon's long brushable hair catches every bit of sunlight, most of the wind.

## Wind & Those Afterthoughts

There are windy days where we think a lot about our hair
This is more likely if our hair is long
Even if it doesn't catch sunlight burning downward
Or doesn't hold darkness in place
The wind likes long hair
Though long hair is not an instrument for the wind to play
Long hair is something to feel and feel
So every stylist loved Rapunzel and the joy she gave
For days after leaving her tower, they forgot the world of tears

## Once In A While

A chicken egg aspires to be a tumbleweed.
A tumbleweed tires of being mistaken for a roving bird's nest.
A bird's nest has an everyday wish for travel.
A grey heron prefers shadowed fresh water to sky.

## Where I'm From

On one side of the river, it always rains
Half the men are named Noah
The sky is a wet pillow

The other side of the river is filled with ne'er-do-well cousins
They are tan from six-days-a-week sunshine
The dress code is hand-me-down suits, boutonniere

Men still fish both sides of the river
No one has caught a fish in a hundred years
Once a month people gather to walk across the water
My grandmother said this started before her mother was a girl

# III.

*yesterday's particle of a parade*

Alfred Starr Hamilton

# Fairy Tale, as a Girl was About to Dream

Brown fox flees storybook
Brown fox runs
Brown fox runs
Running is a way for brown fox
Brown fox's shadow also runs, has a tail
Brown fox's shadow has no scent
Brown fox's fur smells of burnt leaves
Some fire is always burning
Brown fox always finds a fire
Fires burn trails
Ash scent is strong and stays
Embers glow even on starless nights
Brown fox still runs on starless nights
Brown fox runs
Dark birds trill in holes of absent stars

## Spring Day in the Provinces
*for Jeff Gundy*

> *I have hardened my heart only a little.*
> Robinson Jeffers

The first day warm enough for my favorite Hawaiian shirt, without goosebumps.

The fabric, faded and thin. Before I put it on, I check for holes.

Fresh deer tracks beside the mailbox this morning. No time of day I can't hear the interstate's rumblings.

The former governor just said he supports the President, no matter what he does.

If I stop and listen close I hear baby birds crying for worms or warmth in their nest above a back porch column. The father, blue-headed. The mother, all gray. They take turns.

Everything is already green: grass, weeds, trees, and ivy.

A foreign leader stated, "The diversity of our country is actually one of our greatest strengths and a source of tremendous resilience and pride." The White House, surprisingly, offered no comment.

No hard frost in three weeks. That's what the morning weatherman said.

Another governor says this is a time of reflection and prayer. He says everyone should go to church. Then he says he means "house of worship."

A wren is dancing on my neighbor's No Trespassing sign.

"Design thinking" is this week's newsworthy phrase.

Tomorrow I'll take out the tiller for the small, annual work it does. Some years I still find arrowheads. Other years it's just red dirt, rocks, and worms.

## Hitchhiking Towards the Apocalypse

I sat on a rock beside a four lane highway.
The Sunday sun kept me company.
Occasionally, the wind stopped by.

My shirt was faded blue denim.
If my shirt was pond water, the fish could see me.

I had a black-and-white postcard in my shirt pocket.
Every few minutes,
I'd take it out, squint, and pretend it was more than one place.

## Matchstick Hullabaloo

I was setting cars on fire or I wasn't.
I mean, I am setting cars on fire or I'm not.
I have to forget about the past tense.
The past tense is for ghosts and apologists.
Ghosts feed off grievances and errors.
And here, I've never watched a cooking show.
Add that to the bucket list.
Sincere apologists make the best lists.
The best ones name names.
I'm not naming names.
I'm not a good apologist.
I prefer index finger painting, roller coaster screaming,
    or wild flower plucking.
I wouldn't put most of what I want on a list.
There's always some ghost reading over your shoulder.
Even if your shoulders are thick.
I would put the bucket in the car which may or may
    not be on fire.
The bucket won't drive itself.
Some cars will.
We are in the future now.
Ask Jules Verne.
The list is in red ink.
Dorothy's shoes were red and took her to all sorts of
    places.
Her shoes sparkled, sparkled, but were colored differently
    than the ink red list.
Think of flames, licking bright red, etc.
Think of all those places and names.

## The Election

Candidates communicated only by charades.
Slogans culled from Da Vinci's final notebooks.
Protestors on sidewalks wore red crayon sun pendants.
Each vote required something sweet, salty or sour.

Police drug tested all the occupants of clown cars.
The best suicide notes won prizes from the evening news.

## After the Liberation

Bankers gave out autographed samples to whoever asked.
Children wore ink blots as name tags.
Orange trash bags became a fashion accessory.
The number of days in a week varied according to the season.

Art museums featured chalk outlines.
People started saying déjà vu instead of goodbye.
Freeze tag became popular for all ages.
A small minority thought
The moon was a mistake no one could erase.

## Communique

Tomorrow will be like today, only colder.
This is an ongoing pattern.
Ask the crickets still around in late November.
Ask any darkness available for your sleep.

## The Spoils of War

An ashtray filled with thank you notes.
A mounted deer's head, complete with glass eyes and
 wax tears.
Several dented food cans with no labels.
Dried fish bones. Dried duck bones. Dried ox bones.
One poorly printed book of spells.
A few jars for screams. A single cigar box for silence.

## Doomsday Museum

The building is too large to fit in a giant's pocket, but too small for a giant to sleep in.
Tickets are purchased through a local wishing well or by mailing in old obituaries.
The only tour guide is a fortune teller who remains outside.
There's a gift shop, but it's three towns over and closed more than open.
The gift shop is better than the museum.
They have hats and t-shirts.
They have funny, sad refrigerator magnets.
You can leave with a postcard to sincerely mail to yourself.
You can buy a coffee cup to catch good morning sighs.

## The Refugees

Each carries two suitcases:
One for belongings,
One for ghosts.

## Flags Forever at Half-Mast

This is the country you heard rumors about, where quiet weeping is the only sound on the radio and happiness is always past tense, where every decoration includes bullet holes and graffiti and where birds fly backwards to attempt time travel, where angels get lost and give up trying and suicide prevention is in the school's core curriculum, where memory lasts longer than anyone wants, where the sky is a blood orange no one can drink, where a cuckoo clock in each house reminds all citizens when it is time to scream.

## After the Deluge

Fresh from my bathtub gondola, it was a good time to feed
pigeons near the car wash. The sky was blue, as it often is.
I tried to hum a tune stuck at the back of my throat. Most
of what came out sounded like a crow excitedly planning
vacation. Maybe those sounds kept pigeons away despite
Wonder Bread offerings. The day might have been too blue
for them to bother. I could have stayed at home with my
sob pillow, practiced daytime wishful dreaming. I could
have flipped through radio stations to try to find that tune.

## The Man in the Yellow Hat

The man in the yellow hat is gone. He was barely here. They say that about spring in Maine. Then the three days of summer arrive with beetles, bears, and tourists. And who is there to celebrate warmth and cloud breaks with? Not the man in the yellow hat. Let's call him the man with no name who happens to have a big, house paint yellow hat. And let's not forget his pet monkey on a rhinestone leash. Let's at least remember the rhinestones. They would come in handy if we ever played Hansel and Gretel in the forest.

We could take turns being the witch. On the right day, we could forget the way home.

## Not Knowing the Rules

After he was laid off from his job as a hand model, Paul wanted to know what came next. He thought of the unpredictability of slot machines, how they surprise just enough to stay interesting. He thought good marriages are probably like that. Though Paul had never been on a date or kissed anyone other than old relatives at goodbye time. The thought of amorous wonders made his hands sweat, his breath sharp. If those thoughts wouldn't leave, he went to a beach near his house. Very quickly, he could taste salt on his lips.

The beach was often empty. Sometimes he felt he could carry water right into a dream.

## A History of Capitalism

Two cafeteria skeletons fight over a chicken bone. Neither knows the foxtrot or the jitterbug or the hustle or the tango. Little chance the fight will turn into a dance off. Likewise, neither skeleton ever held a rusty cast iron butterfly while it dreamed of flight. All the skeletons know of flight is contained in the chicken bone.

The cafeteria is closed and otherwise empty. The white tile floor mopped to a best left whiteness. Outside, two beggars stand at the window. They call to others on the street to come bet on the action. Soon, they will sell tickets.

## In Defense of Surrealism

The flags we fly are small ones, hand-sewn in another
country. Each made from the emperor's old clothes, so
numerous they fill row-after-row of disused airplane
hangars. He retired years ago to his island with his cotton
candy machine, his pet unicorn, his glitter bomb sling shot,
and his one bookshelf of classic comics. If he was a chicken
he might spend his days crossing and re-crossing the road as
if there was a gun at his back or head or other vital place.
He might ask for rounded pebbles to be scattered in his path
to make a game of his day. Each pebble, he could say, started
as a fallen star.

## Self-Crucifixion

I have trouble doing the last bit. I can place one foot atop the other, nail them down pretty quick. Then my left hand isn't much of a problem. Though I miss the nail a few times because carpentry isn't my skill and because I can't lean over fully, swing all in. The challenge is always my right hand. Once the rest of the work is finished, it waves around unpierced. There's no clean way to nail it myself. I must always cajole some passing stranger through flattery, fetish, or father guilt. Luckily, on a busy street there's always someone willing to step right up and nail it down.

# IV.

*You only know old habits.*
*Who can say they're bad ones?*

Karl Tierney

## People, I Know People

The neighbor who drags a cedar log behind him with a
    rusty link chain
His mother who watches him from her front porch and
    shakes her tiny head
The lady who snorted Ajax because she saw it in a movie
The guy whose ninja skills are reserved for nervous
    breakdowns
The several who dive headfirst into every spider web
Those who love purple wild flowers and stop their cars
    along roadsides to pick them
The ones who've helped me find house and door and
    house key after too many sad drinks
The few who confess hang ups and first thoughts to any
    pair of ears
One fellow with a pet crow and no good story of how that
    came
Another who still hand rolls cigarettes to save money and
    because he likes the discipline
The three or four who make acrobatic shadows as routine
Those who named children after starlets instead of relatives
    Marlena, the only one who named herself

# Leigh

She had a lot of secrets
Some in the pockets of the summer dresses she wore year-round
Some kept out back in an old shed beside oil cans and butt-busted cane chairs
A couple were lonesome in the sugar jar, after she gave up pie
Some were in the blonde first curl above her forehead
One of the secrets was the type of music she kept in her glittery, flapper hat
She kept that hat in the spare closet at the end of a hall she seldom went down

# Sailors

There were sailors everywhere
With sailor white hats
On a bus headed inland

Away from shore, water no longer a mirror,
Nothing seemed endless except sky

The sailor in the farthest backseat drank dark tea
He watched the landscape, wished to be it,
And thought of Alice
And thought of wonderment and heavy dew

When the bus became too noisy
He said hushabye to himself
As though he were his own child

# 13 Things Liz Knows Better Than Most
*for Joel Dailey*

1 .How to enjoy papier-mâché dance shoes
2. Cloud-squaring mathematics
3. The proper way to wear 3 am sunglasses
4. When to blitzkrieg a paradox
5. Favorite dessert servings at the county jail
6. The four steps of passive aggression
7. How to chase surrealist graffiti artists out of the local dump
8. Nullification success stories
9. When to smile in the absence of balloons
10. The best time to quote Dorothy Parker while streaking in a park
11. Flip-flop fashion accessories
12. The transformative nature of the Doppler effect
13. How to win an argument about what tastes best on french fries

## That Same Vincent of Alehouse Fame

If he found wrinkles he called them timelines,
And read between. Firmly believed in survival
Of the sleekest. So he put on makeup when
He kissed up to anyone on stepstool or ladder.
Despite a fear of his own height he played
Through, was well played.
Normally, kisses happened on clean shaven
Days. That was not quite every day
Because of leap year extras. He was always
Pocket-mint fresh, perfumed. So, of course,
He loved daisies. There are over
Twenty thousand daisy varieties.
At night he counted them instead of sheep.
He seldom dreamed of falling, but often of fields.

## Tommy E

Whiskers long enough to make any Texas cowboy or Mississippi catfish envious
Poor enough to live off duct tape and hand-me-down dreams
Gas station hot dogs, his favorite take out
His clothes from a dumpster behind the funeral home
He liked to play harmonica, new tunes fresh from the air
He liked to smoke, even other's leftovers
Often quoted John Wayne and Margaret Mitchell, chapter and verse
Never thought to rope his dog, kick a can, say he was moving

## Lew Welch Going Into the Mountains with His Rifle

He didn't walk all the way to Mexico to see any dancers
He didn't learn how the moon tastes in May rain
Or how to drink the sun off any green leaf

Some paths never circle back no matter how far they stretch
Even paths that reach above the tree line
Where clouds moisten breath

# Sorry

You say that a lot
To the grass before you've taken a step
To the creek running right on top of itself
To any cloud above the glass ceilings of your square glass house

If you owned a sword you would give it away
You could tame fireflies for a whole summer

## Nights & Days

You look all around for a miracle
Just a small one
Something that could break your heart
Then put it back together in a different way

You always loved stories of saints
The sisters told in elementary school
You asked questions by the dozen
Each day, a new candle burned in the window

Once the story was over, you had to pray
The sisters smiled above you
For a full minute they kept count
You tried to whisper absence off your hands

# V.

*something like this day, but not this day*

Stephanie Burt

## Acceptance Jubilee

Once, I mistook my scars for stars and made my own little universe. I was a big boy with my own place. That night was dark. The moon nothing other than far away. So, I measured it with my eyes, fingers, and hands. The measurements varied. Each is private to me. I couldn't settle on any one song to sing to myself. My memory a kaleidoscope of love and grief. The wind stayed gone the whole night. We all know how that is.

## Anyway, It Was In October, I Think

*You can try to make it shorter,* I overheard her say.
I was already late for the bus. And the bus might be early.
So there's a distraction right on the corner.

Distractions are boredom's everyday gifts.
We rush out the door and realize: No keys. No pants.
And, unlike last time, oops, it's not a dream.

It's lovely to see who arrives in our dreams.
Ron and Nancy dropped in. Ronnie was giving a speech.
Nancy was eating a green apple, as she always does.

I never remember what I do in my dreams.
Maybe I'm a clown others pretend not to see.
Maybe I juggle while others talk or eat.

Juggling is not something I can do in waking life.
If I toss something straight up, gravity invariably betrays me.
A good toss postpones betrayal. Late arrivals, be damned.

## Greetings & All

*Goodbye* rhymes with *hi*
For absolutely no good reason.
It's random. The way enlightenment is.
Ask the Buddha or St. Paul if you need a second opinion.

Randomness is a governing principal.
The way random subway strangers meet,
Become something other than.

And how is that?

Well, there's a smile and a chat
And maybe coffee too.

There's that thing some do in daylight and dark,
In bedrooms, broom closets,
And, when the urge is strong or young,
Even well-lit parks.

There's also, sadly, the way things randomly end.
Think of lightening in a summer field, all green fresh
   from rain.

## So Far Away From Tuscany

The day my father taught me how to apply makeup was an important day. Mother too busy chopping wood and practicing her tremulous falsetto. Don't we all have some story to tell? The first bit of astronomy I learned was the location of Venus in the night sky. Sit outside long enough, you'll assign value to whatever you can't reach. Such comforts are important during late night walks and barroom ruinations. No one ever told me to whistle while I work. So I seldom carry a tune more than three daylight steps. That's far enough to impersonate joy. We don't have to be always clowns even if our makeup is badly done. And we can still juggle as if we are. Sometimes shadows might be our audience.

## My Given Name is Mike

I'm making a list of new names for me.
I ask strangers for suggestions.
I give them my card.
It contains my chosen scent and my vital statistics.
It asks them to fill in a blank.

Almost everyone smiles when they read it.
No one has burned a card in front of me.
No one assumes I am a phoenix.
That the remnants of a burning could make eyeliner.
That the name on the blank could be Ash.

## A Slow, Secret Life

Before I began this life, I took a correspondence course
In tiny house repair. Nothing was remembered after a certificate
Was granted. Memory, always the hardest game to play.
My friend, Joe, complains more about it each year. He has
Aged, immeasurably, with sunspots and wisdom, like almost everyone.
I have remained a little girl, thighs powdered white, mimicking
My grandmother's red lipstick poses. Despite it all, my weight
Varies depending on how broken the scale. Possibly every
Wish I've ever made has been over a chocolate bar.
I've met many angels in my most secret life. Each danced
The tango on the head of a needle and dropped rose stems
From their teeth along the way. And there was the time
I met Eileen Myles and loved her, but barely stuttered
More than hello. She gave a hug for knowing who
Jim Brodey was. What I know is small and particular.
My belief system, based on a combination of
Eccentric astrology and traditional Thai spices.
My heart is large, but irregular. Every friend knows when
I miss a beat. So I press leaves in pages of books,
Not yet read, as a reminder that right words are living things.
I somehow never lost my southern accent. Like my voice,
It only deepened with age. People say, I look nothing
Like my pictures. And I sound nothing like the voice
Imagined from a picture frame. It was always like this.
Even when very young and completely hidden behind

The back yard bird bath. That crinkled photo of where I first
Thought to fly. The birdbath always attracted sparrows,
Wrens, and blue jays. They sprinkled me when they bathed.

## Away From the Spotlight, in the July Sun

In those days, my pockets only held lint and lottery tickets.
*Goodbye to You* was my theme song, hummed for at least
One hour a day. My love life based on statistics and poor math skills.
At the time, I was addicted to epiphanies. I found them harder to give up
Than exploding cigars. I was already carrying a dictionary of clichés
As a ready-to-use repository for that moment when original thought
Became too much. Even then the world was
Spinning that way. The calendar told us, along with
What was left of the news. The latest gossip always came from
Street corners and park benches. On Sunday afternoons I would
Stroll the boulevards in my faux pearl necklace with my hair
Braided into a curlicue. Most conversations were
Punctuated by sighs. I supported the idea that a person's
Net worth should be measured by the vowels in her name.
A petition to make that a law went nowhere fast or slow.
Most of my writing paper was leftover invoices. I used
Big old capitalist letters, in block print. I never used cursive
For fear my words would snake into places I didn't recognize
At first glance, which is often the only glance I want to give.
I only wrote in ocean-blue ink with a flamingo feathered pen.
It reminded me romance is possible on some beaches on any day.

# One of Those Times

*stilettos and broken bottles*
                              Robyn

It all began right after my red shoes purchase.
Of course, I'm not talking about the circus kind.
Though those are hard to find, exist only
At specialty shops and fetish clubs. As a
Cafeteria lady once told me, "There's a taste for
Everything." You told me something similar
The first time I opened my purple kimono,
The one awash with peacock imagery,
Trimmed in gold lace.
Yes, subtlety is a bore.
I think that whenever I see a person with a bullhorn
And whenever my bedazzle kit is out of rhinestones.
There are lean weeks when I try to live off
Grocery store samples and cross my toes in hope
Of the big door prize. It's probably just as well my
Wins count to nothing. I carry my losses in my hands,
Ears, and eyes. Many folks have avoided usefulness.
Some collect paper airplanes or boa constrictors.
A few live off dimples, pretend to be wise.

## All the Things I've Got to Do

Make money, of course, a dirty necessity with bills
To pay: plumber for this week's slow leak, along with the
Usual vegetables, bread, rent, and potted plants to keep
Freshness near. Clean refurbished cloth couch of cat hair,
Spare change, taco droppings, and deep buried cotton balls.
Re-watch black and white movies featuring Orson Welles,
Bette Davis, Peter Lorre, Barbara Stanwyck, and
Katherine Hepburn for sure. Find an empty field,
Preferably unused for years. Plant seeds to mimic
Johnny Appleseed. Then go sit, contemplate gravity
Among grass and weeds: how it holds and ages us
All at once. Look for a short mountain to climb, with
A wise prophet half-way up. Ask for wisdom.
Write it down in memory book for handy, quotable use.
Start to read a shelf of Harvard Great Books, that
Library promise to a younger self. Take time to analyze
Fiercely recorded dreams with no censor, open mind.
Oh, yes, relax. Paint toes different colors with crayon box
Inspiration. Go through 64 colors, start fresh again.
Solve each of the world's problems while dancing in
The bathroom, humming, and brushing still short hair.

# Bright Red Calendar Marks

Yesterday was nothing like Easter.
Nothing like Tuesday, which is more recent.
It's easy to be silly, especially if you are a drunk juggler
With no cares about what's missed.
All the jugglers I know are retired or (worse) always sober.
I hope those aren't the only dishes I'm left with.
There's a chance any one of us
Will end with only dreams to serve.
Let me tell you about a dream wish:
When I was a child, John Wayne and Paul Lynde
Took turns watching my crib.
No wolves were ever allowed in.
As a young man, I chopped the crib for firewood.
As it burned, I danced the robot and called it a jig.
What I know of my whole story is somewhere on a
Street corner gathering cold.
There's so little I know.
Who I've met, loved, buried or walked away from
Make not-so-different lists.
So little variety to blush about.
Nothing as exciting as bathroom graffiti.
Not even much compared to overheard remarks
On park walks in spring.

## Some Items Inside That Big Red Box Underneath Your Bed

First childhood phone number.
Least favorite color. (Bruise blue, very popular.)
Misremembered, profanely nonsensical song lyrics.
6th grade heartbreak. (A name is enough.)
Wishful secrets.
Firefly necklace from late night August campfire.
Dream memory of deer antlers in a creek.
Cocoon of barbed wire, long brown hair, and borrowed smiles.
Marilyn impersonations. (Never out of date.)
Flaming moon in open mouths.
A few good lies, just for yourself.
Yellowed map of Appalachia.
Last name of a local ghost.
Burned matchsticks, fresh from a cave.

## Some Fairies

*The fairy who appoints the stars.*

D.R. Wagner

The fairy who flies wingless, but straight
The fairy of snakes, black slithery real and joyfully
    metaphorical
The fairy of concrete nouns, tactile and restful
The fairy of backward numbers, which lead to sleep
The fairy of typos, unexpected messages
The fairy of old hubcaps, shiny at roadside
The fairy of abandonment, garments tossed to the breeze
The fairy of forgotten faces in boxes of photographs
The fairy of O, the world it opens
The fairy who daily trades her sparkling dust
The fairy who daily trades his sparkling dust
The fairy of Grace and Marlena and every proper name
The fairy of player pianos, in tune or not
The fairy of lamps lit in any night window
The fairy of discontinued spells
The fairy of second, third, and fourth chances
The fairy of lost keys

## The Butterfly Mirror I Play Peek-A-Boo With

I might be a matchstick girl who lost her mittens on the mirror's other side. A black cat guards the mittens. The black cat hates Snow White and her perfect teeth.

My mirror hangs steady even when I'm not. On the back of my mirror are B-side lyrics never learned. A butterfly keeps them in place with an hourglass. The butterfly never gets pouty and stays very still. I wish I could live in the hourglass. I'm not at all allergic to sand.

## Dog Sitting

Take dog outside. Take dog back in. Check house for pee and poop. Feed dog.

Use following phrases abundantly: get down, stop, get down, don't chew that, stop, don't eat that, get down, what's in your mouth, come here, don't eat that, what did you get, what is that, don't eat that, I don't know what that is.

Take dog outside. Watch for cats, neighbors, cars. Take dog back in.

Try on collar and leash. Sit on floor with dog in chair. Sleep on floor with dog in bed. Sleep on back and scratch at collar. Whimper with hunger. Whimper at backdoor. Lick backdoor glass. Get excited over falling leaves and flying birds.

Take dog outside. Wear matching collars. Give up leash.

## Autobiography, In Brief

A guy with a glittery mouse collection and a tub of other people's discarded shoes

# Epitaph

He used old stilettos to plant his garden. It was really just an
Onion patch. Mouthwash, aftershave, perfume, and flowered
Ointments hid the smell of his favorite food. As his doormat said,
*What's a Fellow to Do?* Success came with everything not
Related to anything. Outside of money, love affairs, traffic
   tickets,
Beauty supplies, and portion control, his life was charmed.
He held a record for most Pythagoras quotes used when
Ordering a bloody Mary. Friends gave him books on the
   Queen.
Maybe that's why he called butter knives daggers.
No matter, he never complained about bite marks or potluck.
His favorite food was hillbilly porridge. His favorite game was
Glory hole peek-a-boo. His laugh could be heard three
   stoplights
Over. Did I mention he couldn't whisper? Or say the alphabet
   while
You watched? He never offered a cold shoulder to the world.

# It's Lovely, At Last

*for Marko Pogacar*

*To be frank:*
*I didn't owe anyone anything.*
The world came and went without me.
I never put a feather back on a bird,
No matter how bright the sun
Or blue the feather.
All my thoughts happen one at a time
Like an old faucet,
Dripping in an empty house.
When the circus passes,
I go for a walk in the other direction.
Popcorn is bad for teeth, after a certain age.
There's enough salt in a teacup of tears
To suit me, anyway.
If I need more there's the ocean,
Farther away than recent tears.
The ocean is on the other side of the closest mountain.
The mountain is far away, but close to the sky.
I often walk toward the mountain
With my fistful of feathers
Looking for a blue bird.

Mike James makes his home outside Nashville, Tennessee and has published widely. His many poetry collections include: *Journeyman's Suitcase* (Luchador), *Jumping Drawbridges in Technicolor* (Blue Horse), and *Crows in the Jukebox* (Bottom Dog.) He currently serves as an associate editor of *Unbroken*.